CORGI

David Cooke

SHIRE PUBLICATIONS

Published in Great Britain in 2014 by Shire Publications Ltd,
PO Box 883, Oxford OX1 9PL, United Kingdom.
PO Box 3985, New York, NY 10185-3983, USA.
E-mail: shire@shirebooks.co.uk · www.shirebooks.co.uk

A CIP catalog record for this book is available from the
British Library.

Shire Library no. 462 · ISBN-13: 978 0 74780 667 7

David Cooke has asserted his right under the Copyright,
Designs and Patents Act, 1988,
to be identified as the author of this book.

Designed by Ken Vail Graphic Design, Cambridge, UK
Typeset in Perpetua and Gill Sans.
Printed in China through World Print Ltd.

14 15 16 17 18   16 15 14 13 12 11 10 9 8 7

COVER IMAGE
Cover design and photography by Peter Ashley.
Front cover: Corgi Toys No:238 Jaguar Mk10,
1962–1967. With thanks to Paul Marriott. Back
cover: Corgi Toy Model Club badge, collection PA.

TITLE PAGE IMAGE
The first Corgi Toys with original boxes: (from top left)
Morris Cowley, Hillman Husky, Austin Cambridge, Rover
90, Vauxhall Velox, Ford Consul and Riley Pathfinder.

CONTENTS PAGE IMAGE
Very rare gold-plated presentation model of the James
Bond Lotus Esprit, produced for the world premiere of *The
Spy Who Loved Me* on 7th July 1977, mounted on a blue and
black perspex base with a secret drawer for rockets, with a
brass plaque inscribed 'Presented by The Mettoy Co. Ltd.
7th July 1977', and which had an instruction card in its
original gold-coloured display box. According to Marcel
Van Cleemput, only ten of these special models were made,
primarily for important guests at the premiere of the film.

ACKNOWLEDGEMENTS
The author would like to thank all the collectors,
organisations and enthusiasts who have provided him with
information and checked details, especially Marcel Van
Cleemput, Hugo Marsh, John Ramsay, John King, the late
Victor Stowers, Michael Ranson, and the very helpful staff
at Shire Publications. He is also grateful to the following
for the loan of photographs: Hugo Marsh of Christies, Ray
Strutt, Lindsey Amrani of *Model Collector*, Michael Forbes
of *Diecast Collector*, Bryan Goodall of Vectis Auctions and
Brian Salter. The images on page 61 are courtesy of
Corgi ® owned by Hornby Hobbies Limited. Most of all,
he thanks his own family, who have encouraged and helped
him write this book.

**For Marcel Van Cleemput, who encouraged and
consolidated my interest in Corgi Toys.**

Shire Publications is supporting the Woodland Trust, the UK's leading woodland conservation charity, by funding the dedication of trees.

CONTENTS

CHRONOLOGY

1880	Philipp Ullmann born in Germany.
1912	Ullmann establishes the Bechmann & Ullmann toy factory in Nuremberg.
1932	Ullmann emigrates to Great Britain.
1932	Ullmann establishes the Mettoy Company Limited in Northampton (31st August).
1934	Arthur Katz joins the company as company secretary (12th July).
1939	Production turned over to defence contracts.
1941	The production of toys ceases during the Second World War.
1943	Government prohibits sales of toys (30th September).
1944	Mettoy leases newly built factory at Swansea, West Glamorgan.
1945	Cessation of hostilities. Resumption of toy manufacturing.
1948	The introduction of injected moulded toys, including Castoys.
1949	The completed new factory at Fforestfach, Swansea, is officially opened (2nd April).
1954	Marcel Van Cleemput joins Mettoy.
1955	Corgi Toys name suggested by Henry Ullmann (Philipp's son).
1956	Corgi Toys introduced – 'the ones with windows' (9th July).
1958	Major Toys introduced – larger commercial vehicles.
1960	The first of the Chipperfield's Circus items released.
1961	Steering, opening boot and jewelled headlight features introduced.
1964	Original Corgi Classics Cars introduced.
1965	The first television and film related toys and Husky Toys released.
1967	The best year ever for production: over 17 million toys sold.
1969	Factory fire at Swansea with the loss of one year's stock (10th March). Retirement of Philipp Ullmann.
1970	Corgi Juniors introduced – small-scale toys.
1971	Death of Philipp Ullmann.
1978	Special sets produced for Marks & Spencer.
1983	Receivership with debts of £14.5 million (31st October).

1984	Management buy-out. New company called The Corgi Toy Company Limited.	Three film and television related models: the Green Hornet's 'Black Beauty', the *Man from UNCLE* 'Thrush-buster' and the Saint's Volvo P1800.
1985	Shift from mass-production of toys to the adult models market.	
1987	Corgi Classics introduced.	
1994	Introduction of the Original Omnibus Company (OOC).	
1995	The Corgi Toy Company Limited purchased by Mattel. New company called Corgi Classics Limited.	
1996	Mattel merged with Tyco Toys.	
1999	Purchase by Corgi of part of the failed Lledo company including the Vanguards range.	
2000	Corgi acquired by Zindart, based in Hong Kong.	
2006	Fiftieth birthday celebrations.	
2007	Corgi Classics merged with Master Replicas and Cards Inc. to form Corgi International.	
2008	Cards Inc. sold. Hornby Hobbies buys Corgi International for £7.5 million.	

METTOYS – PERFECT SCALE MODELS: 1934–55

CORGI TOYS were the brainchild of a German immigrant, Philipp Ullmann, who arrived in the United Kingdom in 1932. Ullmann was an expert toy manufacturer, having already established a toy business in Nuremberg in 1912 called Tipp & Company (alternatively known as Bechmann & Ullmann). Before coming to England Ullmann had spent seven years in South Africa, where 'he learned many things about many trades'. These would stand him in good stead over the next thirty-seven years. He quickly established a base in Northampton as part of a team that included Frederick Handl and Lionel Gordon, but soon Ullmann became the leading partner of a new company, The Mettoy Company Limited.

Until 1934 he manufactured toys in new premises, but a significant change took place when Arthur Katz, his long-term fellow-director, arrived in July 1934. This entrepreneurial partnership continued until Ullmann's retirement in 1969. He died in 1971. Katz retired in 1980 and died in 1999. While the Hornby family were prospering in Liverpool, manufacturing Meccano outfits, Hornby trains, Dinky Toys and other successful boys' playthings, and the three Lines Brothers were catering for both sexes with Tri-ang Toys and dolls' houses, pedal cars, FROG aeroplanes, Pedigree prams, Minic vehicles, Rovex and a whole host of other creations, Ullmann and Katz were slowly building their own toy empire, Mettoy, based on an exceptional German pedigree. Their production in Northampton continued until the Second World War, when in 1941 the company ceased manufacturing toys.

In September 1943 the Government prohibited the sale of metal toys, stating that no metal model or toy goods, complete or in parts, or castings, would be allowed to be sold, either new or second-hand. It was not until the end of hostilities that the Mettoy factory in Northampton started manufacturing toys again. As well as operating this factory, Mettoy in 1944 acquired a manufacturing factory site at Swansea in South Wales. Following considerable redevelopment, it was officially opened in 1949.

Production recommenced in 1945 with the pioneering of brand-new diecast metal toys. Dinky Toys, manufactured in Liverpool by Meccano since

One of the vehicles in the Castoys series was the Morris delivery van, shown here in the livery of BOAC (British Overseas Airways Corporation).

One of the first post-war Mettoy models, the six-wheeler tinplate lorry with a clockwork motor and steering. This particular model was discovered, in as new condition, in a Welsh toyshop over ten years after its manufacture.

The rather crude label that was attached to these models instead of a box.

1931, at first under the name Modelled Miniatures, established themselves as the leading brand of diecast toys. In the following ten years they assumed a prominent position in the toy trade, although the then relatively small Mettoy Company would over the next thirty years replace Dinky Toys as market leader.

Once the war was over, Mettoy and other toy-manufacturing companies gradually returned to normality. It is significant that virtually all the pre-war makers resumed production of toys and did not turn to other products. Most companies had retained pre-war manufacturing plant on their premises. Rather than spending much-needed capital on new equipment, they modified their existing machines. The late 1940s and early 1950s were years of 'make do and mend', since times were still relatively hard and many items were still rationed. Because of the Korean War, metal was in short supply throughout the world. Hornby, Tri-ang and Mettoy were still in business, the last experimenting with various materials and scales to ascertain which would be most successful. With metal scarce, the company used plastic for the first time. This enabled toys to be made more cheaply and thus to be more affordable. However, the company did not change over completely to plastic. It not only retained its pre-war tinplate production but also followed the lead of Dinky Toys in adopting diecast construction.

By 1948 Dinky Toys were continuing their successful formula of 1/48th scale vehicles. Any rival manufacturer would need to offer something different if he was to compete, and Mettoy responded by producing a series of attractive toys called Castoys, but in a larger scale than Dinky. Introduced in 1948, these models were cast mostly to a scale of 1/35th of the size of the actual vehicle. Compared to Dinky Toys, which were made to an approximate scale of 1/48th and had an average length for small cars, vans and lorries of about 10 cm

One of the very earliest diecast cars, known as Castoys, made by Mettoy in the 1940s. This is the streamlined saloon car, which not only had a clockwork motor but also operational steering.

(4 inches), Mettoy's range appeared gargantuan. The eight vehicles modelled (counting the tractor and trailer set as two) were as follows:

810 Limousine (of unrecognisable make)

820 Streamline bus (single-decker)

830 Racing car

840 Eight-wheel lorry (of unstated provenance, but resembling the then-current Commer lorry)

850 Fire engine

860 Tractor and trailer, forming a set

870 Delivery van (based on the Morris Commercial Z van)

These were the precursors of Mettoy's future toy ranges and most have been seen in various colours. Sales did not approach those of Mettoy's competitors, but production of the lorry and the van continued into 1958, although the remaining models had ceased production by 1951. This series, although uncommon, is not highly collectable today. Some of the later short-lived delivery vans in various liveries do, however, attract high prices at auctions. Mettoy quickly learned that large models require more metal, increasing the costs of manufacture and necessitating a higher retail price.

This motivated Mettoy to produce a new and different range. This time the toys were smaller, and some were made of plastic. The nine models were based on just two prototypes,

Unusual in its day was the Castoys single-decker luxury observation coach with an opening door, as illustrated on its now very rare box.

9

thus reducing production costs and providing lower retail prices. The two vehicles represented were the Rolls-Royce, always popular with children, and the Standard Vanguard, a successful early post-war car already modelled by Dinky Toys. The whole range was introduced in 1951, lasting at least until 1954, and consisted of the following models:

502   Standard Vanguard
505   Rolls-Royce
510   Vanguard police car
511   Vanguard taxi
512   Vanguard Firechief
602   Standard Vanguard
603   Standard Vanguard*
605   Rolls-Royce
606   Rolls-Royce*
*with automatic to and fro bump feature

The toys of the 500 series were all about 7.5 cm (3 inches) long and the 600 series about 11.5 cm (4¹⁄₂ inches) long. Most versions appeared in both plastic and metal varieties, and all contained a clockwork motor. This series, too, failed to catch on, probably because of the dominance of the market by Dinky Toys, which were advertising further varieties in their range.

After these two main experimental series, which hardly made any impact on the young toy-buying public, Mettoy must have decided to emulate their rival. The company was apparently experimenting with various designs to assess their marketability, and the results of this were manifested in their next innovation. This was eventually to propel the company to an unassailable position as the most successful British toy company of its time. So, at the same time that a Dinky Toys look-alike was being produced, Mettoy was registering the name 'Corgi Toys'.

During the 1950s several other British and foreign manufacturers were expanding their production, including Corgi's main rival, Dinky Toys. Among

This large plastic racing car is very rarely seen and is therefore highly collectable. It was made by Mettoy in the early 1950s

others, Matchbox Toys followed up their success with the Coronation Coach in 1953 by producing millions of their small cars. Dinky Toys attempted to introduce their own range of similar toys, called Dinky Dublo, to fit in with the Hornby Trains series, but without major success.

In 1955 a further model was introduced, heralding the forthcoming range. This was a plain red Karrier soft drinks van commissioned by the Co-operative Wholesale Society, with the registration number CWS 300. It was made in diecast metal, like the Castoys from 1948, but, instead of the large scale of the former range, the new van was to a scale of 1/45th and ran on small rubber tyres, just like a Dinky Toy. Doubtless many Dinky Toy fans bought it because of these similarities. Another interesting Mettoy model introduced a few years later, in 1958, was a large-scale Vanwall racing car produced for the Marks & Spencer chain of shops. The fans were in for another surprise, for in July 1956 a brand-new and innovative range was launched, marking a radical change in direction – Corgi Toys.

A very rare trio of Vanwall racing cars produced for Marks & Spencer in 1958. The red and blue versions are particularly rare. These were modelled in 1/18th scale.

An early Corgi retailer's sign.

CORGI TOYS
TRADE MARK REGISTERED

MODEL CAR MAKERS TO
JAMES BOND

155 LOTUS CLIMAX RACING CAR
3½ inches   90mm

CORGI CLASSICS

9013 1915 MODEL T FORD WITH HOOD AND CRANKING FIGURE
3⅜ inches   86mm

314 FERRARI BERLINETTA 250 LE MANS
3¾ inches 95mm

487 CHIPPERFIELD'S CIRCUS LAND ROVER PARADE VEHICLE
3½ inches   91mm

241 GHIA L6.4
4½ inches   108mm

3¾ inches   95mm

325 FORD MUSTANG COMPETITION MODEL

256 VOLKSWAGEN 1200 IN EAST AFRICAN SAFARI TRIM
3⅝ inches   91mm

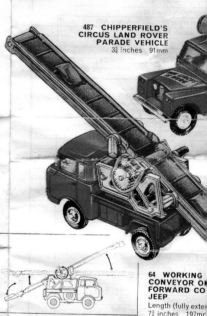

64 WORKING CONVEYOR O FORWARD CO JEEP
Length (fully exte
7¼ inches   197m

Height (fully extended) 14⅝ inches 372mm

CORGI TOYS MAJOR

1127 SIMON SNORKEL FIRE ENGINE
9⅞ inches   252mm

EXPRES

'H' SERIES WITH

'THE ONES WITH WINDOWS': 1956–69

ALTHOUGH Corgi Toys were an addition to the other toys produced by the Mettoy Company, several manufacturers, particularly outside Britain, had already been producing models of a similar diecast design. The idea had been pioneered by Tootsietoys in the United States in the 1930s and was later adapted by Solido in France, Märklin in Germany and, of course, Dinky Toys in Great Britain. All these diecast products, similar in size and scale, proved instantly popular with youngsters throughout the western world.

As well as the huge factory in Swansea, opened in 1949, the Mettoy Company established itself in a new manufacturing complex in Northampton in 1953. Production of their post-war range of toys continued at both sites.

The name 'Corgi Toys' had been invented in 1955, about the time of the Karrier van mentioned earlier, but Mettoy were waiting to achieve maximum market impact with the introduction of the now famous range of toys to which it was to be applied. The company had already used several different names, including Mettoy (*metal toys*), Playcraft (bought in 1954) and Castoys (die*cast toys*) but now needed a simple distinctive name with instant appeal. As one of Mettoy's two main factories was at Swansea it would be fitting if the Welsh connection could be represented in the new logo. It would also be advantageous if the new title were short and sharp in the way that 'Dinky Toys' is. And in 1955, only two years after the coronation of the new Queen, Elizabeth II, she and her family – and their corgi dogs (a Welsh breed) – were constantly in the news. And so, just as 'Dinky Toys' has become a generic term for any small toy vehicles, so 'Corgi Toys' was added to the toy lexicon.

Thus, with a small royal Welsh dog as a logo, Corgi quickly became one of the largest toy companies in Britain, retaining its popularity for a further fifty years. So much for the name; equally important was the product. If anyone at Mettoy had any doubts of success in 1955, by the end of six months' production in December 1956 these would have been completely dispelled. Over 1.3 million toys were manufactured in 1956, and almost three million of the first seven models were produced during their first few years.

Corgi James Bond plans leaflet, showing models in production at the time, together with the words 'Model car makers to James Bond'.

The first seven Corgi Toys with three original boxes: (from top left) Rover, Hillman, Vauxhall, Ford, Riley, Austin and Morris.

Above: The distinctive Corgi logo, used extensively in advertising campaigns.

Right: Corgi Retailers Display.

Three early versions of the Ford Consul, with a later two-tone version on the right.

The person mainly responsible for this success was Marcel Van Cleemput, who had joined the Mettoy Company on 1st January 1954 as a designer and was soon promoted to the position of Chief Designer. In late 1954 he produced the first drawings for the Corgi range and was subsequently involved in every model until the company's demise in 1983.

There were many reasons why these diecast products were successful. There was an extensive range of models; they were often miniature versions of actual vehicles, and all types of vehicles, road, rail, sea and air, were modelled. They were usually small enough to be held in the hand or pocket. Most had freely rotating road wheels so that they could be pushed around easily, and they were often brightly coloured and had an intrinsic charm. Whole series and fleets could be collected. They were strong, well made, lasted almost indefinitely and had considerable play value. They were cheap

Top left:
Two Austin Cambridge cars: original version (top) and later version (below).

Top middle:
More 1950s saloon cars: the Ford Consul in green and the mechanical Riley Pathfinder in dark blue. These boxes contained a concertina catalogue dated January 1957, six months after the launch of Corgi Toys.

Top right:
Two early cars: the Morris Cowley saloon in blue and white and the Lotus MkII racing car in blue-grey, shown with the first-type dark blue boxes.

The company was particularly keen on Vanwall racing cars, especially as the famous racing driver Stirling Moss drove these cars very successfully. They were manufactured not only in the standard scale, as illustrated here, but also in a larger version.

15

Above left: Bedford van, 'Daily Express': the early version of this popular van with plain wheels, original box and split-windscreen.

Above right: Bedford KLG van: another version of this very popular model.

Below left: MGA sports car: one of the first new models in the Sports Car series.

Below right: Ford Zephyr police car. This model has the first-type wheels but also the new features of spring suspension, seats and steering wheel.

A Renault Floride with its special dealer display stand.

Commer dropside lorry: the first new commercial vehicle, which was extremely popular when issued in 1956.

Commer Wall's ice-cream truck. This model also utilises the Commer chassis, with this version having a refrigerated van body.

Below: Karrier Lucozade van, showing the plastic movable shutters on the side.

to buy and were often purchased as birthday or Christmas presents. Corgi Toys would be exported throughout the world. Newly announced models were eagerly awaited by children, and displays and dioramas were suggested in magazines, leaflets and catalogues. Several decades later, many of the small boys who owned these models, now grown into middle age, are filled with nostalgia for these childhood toys, which remind them of the hours of fun that they had manoeuvring buses around the living-room carpet, a fleet of lorries in the sandpit or racing cars in the school playground.

Top left:
Bedford AFS
Utilecon fire
service van,
showing early
wheels and early
box.

Top right:
Shown with their
original dark blue
boxes are the
Hillman Husky in
tan and the
Bedford Utilecon
split-windscreen
ambulance in
cream.

Middle:
Two early light
commercial
vehicles, the RAC
Radio Rescue Land
Rover and the
Bedford Utilecon
fire tender, both
with first-type
wheels.

Bottom:
Three early
commercial
vehicles with first-
type wheels: two
Commers and a
Karrier Bantam.

The old and new boxes with the Studebaker and Ford Thunderbird.

The Donald Campbell 'Bluebird' land speed record car.

Above left: Early fire and police cars with first-type box: Jaguar and Riley Pathfinder.

Above right: Two early cars with first-type wheels: Citroën DS19 (on box) and Standard Vanguard MkIII.

Top left:
The Standard
Vanguard saloon
showing the body,
the windows,
tyres, wheels and
axle together with
the chassis and
gyro motor.

Top right:
A Standard
Vanguard with a
special advertising
display.

The solidly made playthings survived most of those hazardous activities and are much sought after by collectors today, and it is ironic that many of these models, robust enough to have survived to the present day, are now valued at hundreds of pounds and will not venture beyond a display cabinet.

The successful Dinky Toys brand, part of the huge Meccano empire, had cornered the diecast toy market before the war and in the late 1940s the company was reproducing many of its popular pre-war models. Enjoying a virtual monopoly of much of the toy vehicle market, it was set to continue its successful formula. So Mettoy, to be competitive, needed to make inroads into this market. Their immediate success could not be attributed to luck. Typical of a company steeped in Germanic efficiency, their good fortune was the result of strict planning and organisation. Timing was also important, since Dinky Toys were perhaps complacent, believing their huge sales would continue unchallenged.

In 1955 the Dinky Toy range still contained seventeen models that had been designed before the Second World War and only about thirty-five models that had been introduced in the previous three years. There was a ready market for the enterprising. The 1950s model toy collector wanted to own miniature copies of the new vehicles his family was driving or which he had seen in car showrooms. Hence, Corgi carefully selected some of the most popular British cars for their initial range of seven models. Only one duplicated a Dinky Toy and this was probably a coincidence rather than intentional since Corgi's competitor's model was also released in 1956.

The popularity of Corgi Toys was attributable to five factors. First, they were new, modern and different. The Corgi name caught on quickly and Mettoy had an immediate advertising advantage. Second, their aluminium wheels, with a chromium hubcap, looked more realistic than the Dinky Toy painted diecast version. Third, they had treaded tyres, which resembled a real car tyre. Dinky Toy tyres had not altered much in twenty-five years. Fourth, some Corgi Toys were offered with a mechanical gyro motor

Ford Consul Cortina Super estate car with golfing figures.

incorporated in a diecast base, which would enable the car to travel a fair distance when pushed, thus permitting miniature racetracks. The motor's oil filler added to the realistic effect. Dinky Toys still needed a hill for toy races.

Jaguar 2.4 litre saloons: early versions with a pre-1959 blue box (right); later version with spring suspension, seats and steering wheel (left). After 1959 Corgi boxes were produced in the blue and yellow scheme shown on the left.

Left:
The BMC Mini-Countryman in turquoise with surfers and surfboards, and a BMC Mini police van with tracker dog.

The Studebaker Golden Hawk (front) and the Ford Thunderbird.

Above:
Special Golden Guinea gift set comprising the Chevrolet Corvair, Bentley Continental and Ford Consul Classic.

Left:
Rallye Monte Carlo gift set – a very attractive and sought-after set containing the BMC Mini Cooper S, the Rover 2000 and the Citroën DS19.

Two Ford Zephyr estate cars, also showing separate base and construction.

Finally, the most significant feature of all was a simple plastic window insert, making the cars look like their full-size counterparts, and Corgi Toys took full advantage of this in their advertising campaigns by referring to the new range as 'Corgi Toys – the ones with windows'. This marketing ploy proved popular with the toy-buying public. It took Dinky Toys two years to catch up with Corgi; they eventually introduced windows in 1958. Henceforth, Corgi became the market leader, regularly introducing new features months, sometimes years, ahead of their rivals.

Because of the range of different items in the Corgi catalogue collectors throughout the world

Above:
Very unusual when first introduced, the Ford Thames Wall's ice-cream van, complete with canopy and additional figures.

Leaflet for the Wall's ice-cream van, which played the Wall's chimes.

Corgi Model Club
Badge.

A military police van – one
of many military vehicles
that used the original basic
castings.

Four American
cars, all in their
original attractive
yellow and blue
boxes: (from left
to right) Chevrolet
Impala taxi cab,
Ford Thunderbird
Bermuda taxi,
Oldsmobile sheriff
car and Plymouth
Estate US Mail.

Mini-Cooper rally cars
from the 1960s: the 1967
Monte Carlo Rally
winner, version with
roof-rack (left), and
Monte Carlo Rally BMC
Mini Cooper S (right).

Above:
The Lotus Elan: two models, one a coupé, the other a convertible, with sliding windows, opening bonnet, detailed engine and tipping seats. The coupé shows the detachable chassis.

Above:
Three Minis: the Mini Cooper 'Magnifique' (left), and the Surfing Mini (right), together with a basic unpainted body shell.

were keen to extend their miniature fleets. The toys were tough and manufactured in an alloy called Mazak (known as Zamak in the United States), which was virtually unbreakable. The alloy consisted of 96 per cent zinc with small amounts of aluminium, copper and magnesium. The process had been imported from the United States and copied the methods of Dowst, an American company that had made Tootsietoys in the early 1930s. Led by Dinky Toys before the Second World War, British manufacturers excelled in this industry both before the war and into the 1950s and beyond, when they were joined by Corgi, Matchbox and Britain's Toys.

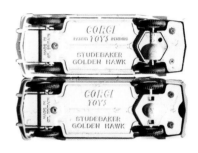

Above:
Studebaker Golden Hawk diecast baseplates; earlier version (upper) and later amended version (lower).

Experiments by Corgi Toys to improve castings and reduce costs over the years resulted in a few models and accessories being made in other materials.

At Mettoy's factory in South Wales huge pieces of expensive machinery were installed to ensure the perfect product. Diecasting is a process whereby molten metal is forced into an extremely accurate die or

Left:
Two Massey-Ferguson tractors: standard tractor (top); version with shovel attached (below).

Top left:
A Corgi Major Toy:
the Bedford Tanker
'Mobilgas' – a
variation of the
articulated tanker
truck.

Top right:
Another Corgi Major
Toy: the Bedford Milk
Tanker. The Bedford S
Type tractor unit was
used with many
different trailers,
including this
attractive version for
milk.

Right:
Three popular ERF
trucks: (from left)
flat truck, cement
tanker and tipper.

Special Corgi
collectors' case
containing a
portable service
station.

Top:
Special Commer promotional van in blue, white and green made for Hammonds of Hull.

Middle:
Three cars of the 1960s showing opening parts: Aston Martin, Bentley Continental and Ghia.

Bottom:
Aston Martin DB4s with opening bonnets, engines, seats and spring suspension.

27

Top left:
With the popularity of the Concorde airliner, Corgi produced several versions of the plane, this one in Japan Air Lines livery.

Top right:
Probably the most successful Corgi Toy of all times was the Land Rover (left), with several million produced in many different versions. The highly detailed Massey-Ferguson combine harvester appeared in the Corgi Major series.

Middle:
A Rover 2000: the complete model with instructions, together with the several parts and a set of interchangeable wheels.

Bottom:
The Rover 2000, illustrating the detachable spare wheel.

Extremely popular, particularly as special presents, were the car transporters with cars, which appeared throughout the Corgi Toys production period. Illustrated is the Ford transporter, together with a Rover, a Hillman, a Ford and three Minis.

Left: Farm gift set: Ford 5000 Super Major tractor with driver and working conveyor on trailer.

Below right: Two buses from the 1960s: (top) Holiday Camp Special Commer bus with roof rack; (below) Midland Red motorway express coach, which appeared in the Corgi Major series.

Below left: Sports and rally cars, including (from top) the Porsche Carrera, Lotus Elan, Volkswagen 1200, Hillman Hunter and Cooper-Maserati.

The gift sets were popular for Christmas and birthday presents. This set contains three Lotus cars with their transporter.

mould; when it has solidified and cooled the resulting castings are trimmed, cleaned and enamelled.

The toys were painted in bright, sometimes unrealistic colours and could be identified by the name Corgi Toys and/or the model name and number on the chassis. The model was then packed in its own box, or occasionally as part of a gift set, for further identification and protection. The cardboard and later plastic boxes varied considerably over fifty years. Early boxes, particularly those for the film and television series, are very

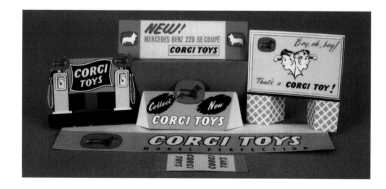

Advertising material for Corgi Toys.

A Corgi Major Toy: the second version of the Bedford Carrimore car transporter with lift-off lid box.

Another Corgi Major Toy: the Karrier radar control – a very unusual and complicated model with working radar unit.

rare and much sought after by collectors.

The finished products were then dispatched to the retailer, who was supplied with Corgi Toys marketing material to display the toys. Merchandising items such as glass cabinets, catalogues, price lists and special metal price tags were made available to the dealer, whose shelves would have been kept well stocked with boxes of Corgi Toys.

With regards to size and scale, the majority of the earlier Corgi Toys cars were around 10 cm (4 inches) long, with the larger and more expensive models known as Corgi Major Toys (mostly trucks, lorries and construction equipment) up to 30 cm (12 inches) long. However, in 1965 Corgi Toys launched a series of smaller models, entitled Husky Toys. These were

A very attractive pictorial illustration of one of the popular farm sets that were much sought-after at Christmas.

Gift set containing a Volkswagen breakdown truck and trailer together with a blue Cooper-Maserati.

Large gift set 15, the Silverstone racing layout.

Three Minis: (from left) the BMC Mini Cooper S, winner of the Monte Carlo Rally in 1967; the BMC Mini Cooper S, winner of the 1966 RAC-Sun International Rally; a Morris Mini Minor in metallic maroon.

followed in the 1970s, in an effort to expand the business, by toys that were produced in larger scales. Cars were 1/36th scale, measuring around 15 cm (6 inches) long. Sizes of the other toys varied considerably, from the smallest aeroplanes, for example a Boeing 747 Jumbo Jet measuring about 15 cm (6 inches) long, to a very large combine harvester.

A typical Corgi model was made up of three or more parts; the fewer the parts, the cheaper it was to produce. A basic model car of the late 1950s consisted of a one-piece diecast body, originally with a tinplate chassis, to which were attached two metal axles, turned aluminium wheels, rubber tyres and the plastic window section. However, shortly after introduction of the range, the chassis too was diecast (and much later some were made of plastic). The

A Routemaster bus in red, advertising Corgi Classics.

Corgi often produced limited edition versions for companies. This Austin Seven Mini was made for Jensen's of Denmark and is now very rare.

Below left:
A Routemaster bus. This very rare version was produced for the Australian market, finished in an unusual green livery, advertising Corgi Classics.

Below right:
One of the rare limited edition Routemaster buses with Red Rose Coffee advertisements.

chassis also bore the manufacturer's name and brief details of the model. The body, chassis and windows were riveted together. There are exceptions to this system, but this holds good for the majority of Corgi Toys.

More expensive models, such as the Corgi Major Toys, consisted of two body parts: the cab and chassis from one mould, and the container component in the other, together with a smaller baseplate beneath the cab.

In the following decades techniques improved so much that the manufacturing process included a complete diecast or plastic chassis, many other plastic parts such as seating, wheels and grilles, together with an

enormous variety of operating items like doors, bonnets, tipping mechanisms, cranes, elevators and even flashing direction indicators. These sophisticated toys had come a long way from their basic humble beginnings in 1956. Prices, however, remained within the reach of children, for whom they were intended. During the late 1950s the average price was about 3 shillings (15p) for small cars, 5 shillings (25p) for lorries, rising to 10 shillings (50p) for some smaller sets and an enormous 35 shillings (£1.75) for a large gift set consisting of four pieces.

In 1965 the company moved into top gear with a complete change of direction, devoting much of its production to models relating to films or television programmes. These models are the subject of a separate chapter. During the late 1960s Corgi Toys were at the peak of their production, and twenty-two models achieved sales of a million or more in the period from their launch up to 1983.

Six of these were film or television related and many were released or available during the years 1970 to 1980; however, only one, the James Bond Lotus Esprit (no. 269), lasted beyond 1983. The best-selling model car outside the film and television category was the John Player Special (JPS) racing car.

The models in the list on page 37 represent a good cross-section of popular British, European and American cars, emergency vehicles such as a fire engine, an ambulance and a police car, racing cars, farm vehicles and a bus. There were three unusual entries. The first, the Ghia L.6.4, was rarely, if ever, seen on British roads, since only six full-sized cars were produced. However, it was the fourth best-selling Corgi Toy, owing its popularity as a model to its special new features, remarkable when introduced in 1963, of

One of the best-selling Corgi toys, the Ghia L.6.4.

American Cadillac Superior ambulance with flashing light.

Three Jaguar Mark X saloons in light blue, silver and metallic blue, which contained luggage in their boots, 'By Special Request'.

four opening parts, tip-up seats, jewelled headlights, plated parts, detailed engine, suspension, a hidden bonnet latch and a dog lying on the rear parcel shelf. All this, for 8s 6d, accounted for one million sales in its first two years and a massive 1.75 million in total. The other unusual entries were the two versions of the Land Rover breakdown truck. The first, no. 417 (planned

Three tractors with accessories in the distinctive Corgi blue and yellow boxes: Massey-Ferguson 165 tractor with saw attachment, Ford 5000 Super Major tractor with hydraulic scoop, and Ford 5000 Super Major tractor with trenching bucket.

Production (millions)	Model number	Model	Production (millions)	Model number	Model
4.9	267	Batmobile (F)	1.4	477	Land Rover breakdown truck
4.0	261	James Bond Aston Martin (F)	1.3	437	Cadillac Superior ambulance
2.0	154	John Player Special racing car	1.3	154	Ferrari F1 racing car
1.7	241	Ghia L.6.4	1.2	270	James Bond Aston Martin (silver) (F)
1.7	226	Mini Minor	1.2	1127	Simon Snorkel fire engine
1.7	438	Land Rover	1.2	258	The Saint's Volvo (F)
1.6	233	Heinkel bubble car	1.1	211	Studebaker Golden Hawk
1.6	314	Ferrari Berlinetta	1.1	238	Jaguar Mark X saloon
1.5	269	James Bond Lotus Esprit (F)	1.1	223	Chevrolet State Patrol
1.5	497	The Man from UNCLE (F)	1.1	53	Massey-Ferguson tractor shovel
1.4	468	London Routemaster bus	1.0	417	Land-Rover breakdown truck (first version)

Source: *The Great Book of Corgi* by Marcel Van Cleemput. (F) = film or television related.

N.B. Nine of the above (models 267, 438, 233, 314, 468, 154, 270, 1127 and 258), whose sales continued after 1968, sold even more than indicated, as sales records were lost in a disastrous fire at the Swansea factory on 10th March 1969.

Five Citroëns in various guises: three Safari estate cars (top) with the 'Le Dandy' coupé (left) and the DS19 saloon (right).

Above: Austin driving school cars: the British version on the left, and the version with left-hand drive on the right.

Right: Box for the Austin Cambridge driving school car with special leaflet.

A set from the extensive and sought-after Chipperfield's Circus series, illustrating the crane truck, various trailers, a booking office and a Land Rover.

This specially produced Volkswagen van, a limited edition labelled for the Dutch company Vroom & Dreesmann, is now particularly rare.

no. 410), introduced in 1960 with a metal canopy, was renumbered 477 in 1965 when it acquired a plastic canopy. So in practice they can be regarded as the same model, with total sales of over two million – even more than the JPS racing car.

The Simon Snorkel fire engine, always a favourite with children, was the best-selling Major Toy, and the Daktari set (containing yet another Land Rover) only just fell short of a million sales, making it the best-selling set. The Land Rover in all its guises (pick-up, breakdown, RAC, RAF, Chipperfield's Circus), with total sales of over ten million, far outsold every other Corgi model, even the James Bond Aston Martin.

Five Land Rovers: (from left) early RAC version, two breakdown service vehicles, Classics range RAC radio patrol, and an Edinburgh Corporation service van.

THE FINAL YEARS OF MASS PRODUCTION: 1970–85

FOLLOWING the very successful years of the late 1960s, when total sales hovered around the 15 million mark, competition from other manufacturers was beginning to bite and the 1970s were to bring reduced production. Dinky, producing similar toys to Corgi, were still a force to be reckoned with, although their output was much reduced. Furthermore, a new challenger, this time from America, had appeared on the scene and threatened to eliminate both companies and perhaps Matchbox Toys as well. A new range from Mattel, one of the largest toy companies in the world at that time, was named Hot Wheels and had been introduced in 1967. Matchbox Toys had been the first to suffer directly from the American broadside, since Mattel's products were of a similar size. Unusually, Dinky Toys had stolen a march on Corgi with the new wheels, Dinky being more often the follower of Corgi's lead. Dinky had introduced its Speedwheels in June 1969, with Corgi following in September and October with its own version, called Whizz Wheels.

Mattel had cleverly designed a new axle and wheel combination that would ensure that, when pushed, the toy would not only travel further but also faster. A much thinner axle was used (with Mattel's toys it was as thin as a pin), together with lightweight smooth all-in-one plastic wheels, instead of the usual practice of a diecast wheel fitted with a rubber tyre. Matchbox had introduced Superfast wheels, and Dinky Speedwheels. However, Corgi countered with not just one but two new features, Whizz Wheels and Corgi Rockets. First, in September 1969, came Whizz Wheels, which were a direct challenge to the other manufacturers. These were followed in October by Corgi Rockets, a unique and sophisticated system that led to other accessories being available with the toy itself. Cars with Rockets were fitted with a detachable nylon frame called a sub-chassis, which incorporated the new Whizz Wheels. The various parts of the frame could be removed for more play value. In addition, complicated tracks were produced to enable the initial series of seven cars (Matchbox-sized) to propel themselves up, down, round and round just like a roller-coaster. The seven Rockets cars, all previously in the Husky range, were soon to be renamed Corgi Junior.

Opposite page:
A selection of six models from the 1980s based on 1950s classic cars. At the top is a Jaguar XK120, and underneath it an MG TF; at front left are a Rolls-Royce Silver Dawn convertible and a Mercedes Benz 300 SL; and at front right are a Jaguar XK120 and a Bentley 'R' Type.

Top left:
Four Minis with
WhizzWheels.

Top right:
WhizzWheels,
fitted to the
Morris Marina,
Ford Cortina and
Mini.

Another reason for the urgent need for WhizzWheels was that the company not only had to compete with Mattel in Britain, but also in the important export markets, especially the United States, where the American company naturally had an established hold. In 1967, over 55 per cent of Corgi's production was sold abroad. Whether the delay in introducing these two new ranges was due to a factory fire in March 1969 or to the complexity of the Rocket range is not known, but the loss of a few months' production did not appear to cause the company too many problems.

From 1970 onwards nearly all the new cars, but not commercial or other types of model, would be fitted with WhizzWheels, much to the annoyance of avid model collectors, who deplored the loss of authenticity. However, Corgi Toys were in the business of producing toys for youngsters, who were their main market, and not for the smaller model-collecting fraternity.

One of the models
that sold a million,
the very popular
Lotus John Player
Special racing car
in black and gold.
This is a model of
the Lotus that
became the
Formula 1 World
Championship
racing car of 1972.
The box has a
detailed
description on the
back and also gives
information about
Ronnie Peterson,
the driver.

The later, larger, Routemaster Bus, introduced in 1975. This rare version, produced in May 1977, was specially made for the visit of Swiss buyers to the Swansea factory.

Forty-one new models were introduced in 1970, including many cars that were conversions of older models to WhizzWheels, but allocated new numbers and given new paint finishes. There was also a tri-decker car transporter, a fictitious Lunar Bug and a handful of other vehicles.

Farm models in window boxes: the Land Rover and Rice's Beaufort double horse-box gift set; Ford 5000 Super Major tractor with hydraulic scoop; and Mercedes-Benz Unimog with goose dumper.

Six aircraft in clear-plastic-topped boxes, which were very popular in the 1970s: (from top left): Swissair Douglas DC-10; British Airways Vickers VC-10; British Airways Boeing 747 Jumbo; three North American P-51D Mustangs in different liveries.

Three 1/36th scale Corgi cars from the late 1970s and early 1980s. From left: a Rover 3500 police car, a Jaguar XJS 'TWR' and a Lotus Elite.

Apart from WhizzWheels, another significant development was the reintroduction of smaller Matchbox-sized models. Husky Toys had first been released in 1965 to compete directly against Matchbox Toys, but they had been sold exclusively through the F. W. Woolworth chain of shops. After this arrangement ceased in 1970, Corgi renamed the range 'Corgi Juniors'. With the conception of Rockets, Corgi took the opportunity of re-establishing the range of smaller-scale toys, all featured in a catalogue when the new series of Corgi Juniors was announced. During that year over fifty of these small vehicles were launched, this time with distribution through normal Corgi outlets. Rejigged versions of the old Husky toys included not only conventional vehicles but also miniature examples of popular film and television related models such as the James Bond Aston Martin, Chitty Chitty Bang Bang, the Batmobile and the Monkeemobile, which also had appeared briefly in the Husky series. Yards of special Rocket track were also produced to complement this very wide range of toys. Dinky Toys' contribution to this sector of the market was short-lived, with the Dublo series, lasting only from 1957 to 1967, and a set of Mini Dinky Toys manufactured in Hong Kong.

Like other toy manufacturers, Corgi Toys were experiencing intense competition during the late 1970s. The Lines Brothers empire, which included Dinky Toys, already inherited from Meccano in 1964, was itself taken over by Airfix Industries in 1971. In 1979 the Dinky factory in Liverpool closed.

By that year other factors had entered the equation, with higher interest rates, wage rises and a strong pound putting pressure not only on Corgi but on their suppliers, as well as their own dealers. Profits dropped by £1.5 million. 1980 was even worse, with the first trading loss since 1971 – nearly £3 million. Staff were made redundant, units were closed and sales fell by over 3.5 million items. With a loss in 1981 of £2.4 million, £4 million in

Rob Walker racing car and 1973 catalogue.

1982, and more redundancies, the company could not continue and in October 1983 Mettoy called in the receivers.

Dinky Toys had disappeared in 1979, Dunbee Combex Marx in 1980, Airfix in 1981, Lesney (Matchbox Toys) in 1982 and Berwick Timpo in 1983. Factors influencing the demise of these toy manufacturers included a decline in child population, the recession, increased competition from abroad and the expansion of video and computer games.

However, a ray of hope enabled the company to continue manufacturing and trading to the present day. In early 1984 a management buy-out acquired all the tools, machinery and work in progress as well as the remaining stock. The new company was called 'The Corgi Toy Company Limited'.

The beginning of a new era, celebrating the launch of the new Corgi Company on 29th March 1984.

45

FILM AND TELEVISION
RELATED TOYS: 1965–82

CORGI TOYS' most successful period of manufacturing was between 1965 and 1968, when over 60 million toys were sold. During the peak year of 1967 over 17 million were produced. These dates coincided with the timely introduction of film and television related toys. Current films and television programmes that featured distinctive vehicles were exploited, with miniature versions of these vehicles produced for the toy trade. Corgi Toys were particularly adept at this character merchandising and stole a march on their competitors. Dinky Toys managed to obtain the rights to only one major series, *Thunderbirds*, plus a handful of smaller television personalities, for its contribution to this genre. Although beaten by Dinky for the *Thunderbirds* licence, Corgi captured such famous names as James Bond, Batman, *The Man from UNCLE*, the Saint, Wooster, Chitty Chitty Bang Bang, the Beatles, Popeye, Noddy and many other characters popular between 1965 and 1982.

The first famous car to be miniaturised, in 1965, was the Saint's Volvo P1800 sports car, which would sell well over one million models. This was closely followed by the first of the James Bond Aston Martins in October 1965, a specially released model aimed at the Christmas market. This model turned out to be Corgi's most successful toy car – even though it was finished in gold paint, rather than the film's silver – with total sales just short of four million, three quarters of a million being sold in the last few months of 1965. Subsequently, there was a shortage of the Aston Martin in toyshops, and even Hamleys, the huge Regent Street toyshop in London, had sold out by November. Corgi's Advertising Manager, Bill Baxter, said: 'We never in our wildest dreams expected such phenomenal sales.'

This model, no. 261, was the first of several James Bond Aston Martins. Further Aston Martins followed in 1968 (no. 270, in silver), in 1978 (no. 271, also in silver) and even more in the 1990s, as nostalgic collectors' items, providing total sales of over five million of probably the most famous model car in history. It was little wonder that Dinky Toys closed their factory in 1979, just a year after the third Aston Martin was released by Corgi. They could not keep up with such intense competition.

Opposite:
Television-related
models: Basil Brush
in his Renault
(top); the *Avengers*
set, containing a
Bentley coupé and
a Lotus Elan.

The *Man from UNCLE* car: an unusual version in white; they were normally dark blue. It shows clearly the Waverly Ring, an essential part of this set.

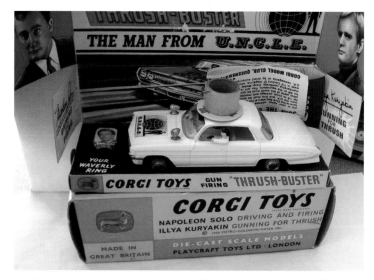

Two film and television related models: the James Bond Toyota 2000 GT with missiles, and the metallic blue 'Thrush-buster' from *The Man from UNCLE*.

Corgi worked very closely with the producers of these films and television programmes, and for the James Bond Lotus Esprit issued in 1977 Marcel Van Cleemput, Corgi's Chief Designer, was summoned to Pinewood Studios by the film producers to discuss the model of the latest Bond car.

Corgi quickly realised that they had discovered a gold mine with these film-related models and took full advantage of their prominent position by releasing the toys in the table on page 51, amongst others, during the late 1960s and through the 1970s.

Left:
The Saint's car –
the Volvo P1800
with rare red
bonnet label.

Very collectable
James Bond Aston
Martin DB5s – the
original gold
version and the
later silver
version.

49

Extremely popular with children, the ingenious Chitty Chitty Bang Bang in both normal and Husky versions.

During the 1970s many television programmes were the subjects of miniature toy manufacturing, including this extensive set of figures featured in *The Magic Roundabout*.

Of the twenty-two individual Corgi models selling over one million items over the years, six were character based, such as the Batmobile (no. 267). However, the James Bond Aston Martins were the most successful Corgi Toy cars ever, with sales of over five million between 1965 and 1979. A further twenty-eight film-related models were introduced up to 1982, but by this time Corgi, like other toy companies, was suffering, and with sales down to 4.5 million per annum (from a peak of 17 million per annum) the company was unfortunately heading for collapse.

No.	Model	Date	No.	Model	Date
258	Volvo Saint	1965*	801	Noddy	1969
261	James Bond Aston Martin	1965*	802	Popeye Paddlewagon	1969
497	*The Man from UNCLE*	1966*	808	Basil Brush	1971
267	Batmobile	1966*	811	James Bond Moonbuggy	1972
9004	*World of Wooster*	1967	925	Batcopter	1976
336	James Bond Toyota	1967	290	*Kojak*	1976
270	James Bond Aston Martin	1968*	269	James Bond Lotus Esprit	1977*
266	Chitty Chitty Bang Bang	1968	292	*Starsky and Hutch*	1977
803	Yellow Submarine	1969		* Sold over one million toys	

This table illustrates the popularity of film and television related toys. Well over 30 individual models were produced, with total sales reaching many millions. The 17 listed here sold over 18 million in total, with the James Bond vehicles sweeping the board.

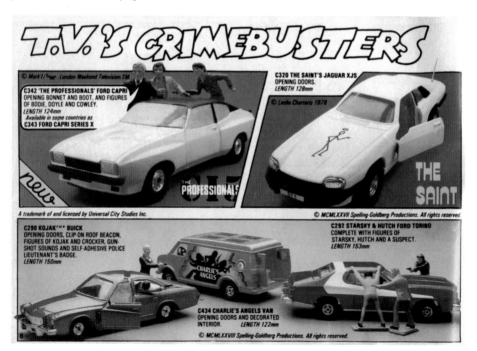

'T.V.'s Crimebusters', from the 1979 Corgi catalogue.

Duckham's Oils
Perfection in Lubrication
LONDON BIRMINGHAM GLASGOW

WAKEFIELD *Castrol* MOTOR OIL

ST. CANNON STREET, LONDON
TELEPHONE No. 572
ESTD 1899

C⭕RGI *Classics*

821
1929 Thornycroft Van

SAFEWAY
ESTABLISHED 1926
PURVEYORS WORLDWIDE
QUALITY PROVISIONS, FRUITS, WINES

Safeway Food Stores Limited
Aylesford Kent

This is a Collector's
model produced
as one of a
strictly limited
edition

Limited EDITION

C⭕RGI *Classics*

CORGI CLASSICS: FROM 1985

FOLLOWING the management buy-out of Corgi Toys during the 1980s, the company decided to move away from the mass-production of children's toys, with all the associated headaches of manufacture, fashion and distribution, to concentrate on the adult collectors' market. This process began in 1985, when a new range of Classic Commercials was introduced and featured in that year's forty-eight page catalogue. At the same time four models from the original Corgi Classics car range of the 1960s were reintroduced – a Rolls-Royce, a Bentley, a Renault and a Model 'T' Ford. The first of the Corgi Classics Commercials range was a vintage Thornycroft in van and truck guise and was the precursor of a huge and varied collection. The first twenty-five or so Thornycrofts, released in 1985, were joined by a further fifty with similar chassis but with completely different advertising, ranging from Shell Oil to Sandringham House, and by almost 250 other individual designs. These covered such fields as: trucks and vans with advertising; buses, both British and foreign; emergency vehicles; cars; military vehicles; film and television related items; French vehicles; traction engines; circus vehicles; trams; and one of Corgi's latest ventures, aeroplanes (named the Aviation Archive). Over 250 designs have provided more than two thousand individual items, which were all separately numbered, commencing with C820, the Thornycroft East Anglian Fruit Company truck, through the 800 and 900 series of numbers, continuing with five-figure numbers such as 98101 (previously C983/5), the Morris Wall's ice-cream van, introduced in 1991. The revised numbering system survives to this day. One model that has had many variations in design is the Morris Minor van and pick-up, which has been produced in at least seventy different liveries since its introduction in 1987, beginning with no. C957, made in England, and through to, for example, no. 06507, a BRS parcels van made in 1999 in China, which is already highly sought after. These delightful models are mainly manufactured in 1/43rd or 1/50th scale, although the aeroplanes for obvious reasons are in 1/72nd or 1/144th scale.

Three Thornycroft vans from the 1980s in Duckham's Oils, Castrol Oil and Safeway Stores liveries. These were designed to compete with Lesney Yesteryear vans.

An open-top City bus was available on a similar chassis to the Thornycroft vans shown in the background.

A major exception to these scales is the Original Omnibus Company series of buses and coaches, which are in 1/76th scale (OOC – 'OO' indicating the Hornby Dublo scale of toys dating back to before the Second World War). The finely detailed vehicles appeared on the scene later than the commercial vehicles mentioned previously, in response to a range of

Two Morris Minor vans: Royal Mail and Post Office Telephones.

buses in the same scale by another manufacturer, Exclusive First Editions (EFE). This company still makes many thousands of very accurate models of British buses in a popular sector of the market. EFE vehicles first appeared in 1989 and were an immediate success with collectors. Corgi responded some five years later but within another five years had caught up with EFE and was producing models of similar quality and, much to the annoyance of some collectors, similar models. The production of the wartime Guy Arab Utility double-decker bus by both companies was felt to be superfluous, but it did at least give collectors an opportunity for a strict comparison of the two models. Most collectors concluded that there was little to choose between the two companies, each producing excellent results. Corgi has released well over fifty individual designs with more than a thousand different liveried buses and coaches.

Three Eastern Coach Works double-deckers from the Original Omnibus Company, introduced in the 1990s: (from left) two Bristols and a Leyland – buses from the Tilling Group of companies.

Corgi usually introduces around twenty new models each month, covering most of the desired categories, i.e. commercial vehicles, traction engines, Original Omnibus Company and the Aviation Archive.

Model collectors, as opposed to toy collectors, have different priorities, since they require greater authenticity from their replicas. The trucks, vans and buses, which are the classes of vehicle that are mainly collected today, are produced by Corgi Classics and other manufacturers for adult collectors who have no intention of playing with the models but display them neatly in cabinets as soon as they are purchased.

By the year 2000 Corgi Classics Limited was advertising: 'Each 1/50th scale model ... has been carefully researched ... a true representation of the original ... to give the collector and enthusiast .... Each model contains upwards of 40 parts and up to 150 precision applied printing operations ... includes a numbered Limited Edition Certificate.' There was no mention of the word 'toy' in a two-page coloured advertisement, since very few of these

Above:
Four models from the late 1990s of British Road Services trucks in their splendid red livery: (from left) Bedford 'S' Type articulated; AEC Mammoth Major; ERF eight-wheel platform lorry; Foden FG eight-wheeler.

latest models will fall into children's hands. Back in the late 1950s, 200,000 Jaguar 2.4 saloons were sold in one year alone; today a limited edition of an individual model of a Corgi Classic bus (for example) will sell exactly two thousand and no more. The difference is that most of the Jaguars ended up in toy boxes and became almost worthless, whereas all the buses, exhibited in their cabinets, will remain in perfect condition, complete with their original packaging, and should at least retain their former retail value. It is unlikely that the overall average value of these models will increase at the same rate as old toys have in the past, because

Five British sports cars: (from top left) Jaguar XK120, MGA, Austin-Healey 100-Six, Jaguar E-Type, Triumph TR3.

all the models will remain in mint-boxed condition. Those collectors who sought that model for their collection would have purchased it when it was released. A few collectors, new to the hobby, may wish to purchase older issues, but this should not mean that values will soar. A few of the models released will increase in value, but being able to spot in advance which they will be is almost impossible. On the other hand, thousands of remaindered models regularly appear at toy auctions, selling at well below their original retail price. So, if the model is for potential investment, let the buyer beware.

Four large vans from the late 1990s: Bedford 'Spratts', Thames 'Heinz', Thames 'Ever Ready', Bedford 'Weetabix'. Based on Dinky Toys' large vans first introduced in the 1940s, they celebrated forty years of Corgi Toys production in 1996 and paved the way for the huge development of specially liveried trucks.

THE TWENTY-FIRST CENTURY

L ARGE toy companies, particularly those based in the United States, are always on the lookout for opportunities for expansion and development; and the acquisition of successful smaller organisations can provide such opportunities. Thus, in 1995, the giant American conglomerate Mattel took over the Corgi company, which then became known as Corgi Classics Limited. And a year later, in 1996, as if to illustrate the complexities of the toy industry, Mattel then merged with Tyco Toys. Tyco had acquired the Dinky Toys name in 1992 and so, for a time, Corgi and Dinky were in the same stable.

In addition to the previously mentioned ranges, which are now well established, the company expanded after purchasing the name and part of the manufacturing and design division of another British toy company, Lledo. Lledo had been the brainchild of Jack Odell OBE, a distinguished diecast engineer who had been a director of Matchbox Toys until that company also encountered financial difficulties. Lledo (Odell spelt backwards) had from 1983 until 1999 established an impressive range of toys, called Days Gone, Promotionals, View Vans and Vanguards, which attracted a huge following of

Detailed models of (left to right) the MG ZT, Rover 75, police Range Rover, Jaguar XJR and the Vauxhall Astra.

Eleven British Vanguards, including Rovers, Fords and Hillmans.

Twelve British classics from the Vanguards range, including Fords, Vauxhalls, Rovers and Triumphs.

Five British modern classics from the Vanguards range: (from top left) Ford Zephyr, Vauxhall Victor, Morris 1100, Austin A60, Austin Allegro.

Assorted police cars from the Vanguards range, including Fords, Vauxhalls, a Rover and a Jaguar.

model collectors. Like Corgi Toys, Lledo experienced financial troubles and the company ceased production in 1999. Corgi Classics quickly came to the rescue, soon reintroducing some of the existing Lledo range, as well as expanding and releasing new models in the ranges, much to the delight of model collectors. More changes took place in 2000, when both the Corgi company and Lledo were acquired by Zindart, a large diecast manufacturer based in Hong Kong. Production is now predominantly in China.

As well as producing models for the adult market, the company has now turned full circle and is also again manufacturing toys for children. The limited range consists mainly of vans, trucks and buses that utilise existing components and are therefore cheap to produce and can be priced to suit the children's market. These Corgi Toys, together with another range called Motoring Memories, are presumably aimed at children so that as they grow up they will be attracted to the more expensive models in the Corgi Classics range and remain customers for years to come.

Corgi retains a large slice of the British toy and model market and have successfully fended off competition. The adult market shows no sign of

A selection of five magnificent Vauxhall Cresta PA saloon cars produced for the Vanguards series around 2000, with original boxes (at front) and new-style boxes (top). All are in 1/43rd scale.

The Monte Carlo Rally Set, a fine example from the Vanguards series, modelled at 1/43rd scale.

weakening, with many collectors purchasing all the new releases every month, which amounts to a considerable sum of money. The future looks good for Vanguards, while the existing ranges will, no doubt, continue to expand.

Mettoy, Castoys, Corgi, Husky, Mattel, Tyco, Zindart, Corgi International, and in 2008, Hornby Hobbies. On 1st May 2008, the well-known toy and model company, Hornby, announced the purhase of Corgi for £7.5 million. Frank Martin, the Chief executive of Hornby, explained, 'it is a fantastic brand and has a superb reputation worldwide. We intend to build its premier position in the market.'

Since Mettoy commenced business in Northampton in 1932 and Corgi Toys were introduced in 1956 the company has experienced continuous production, albeit under several different owners, and has enjoyed considerable success, particularly during the boom years of the late 1960s; it has suffered financial difficulties through changing fashion but has nevertheless managed to survive and continues to produce delightful, accurate scale models, for future generations to enjoy.

The first Corgi model produced after the Hornby takeover in 2008: a Series 1 Land Rover produced in celebration of Land Rover's sixtieth anniversary.

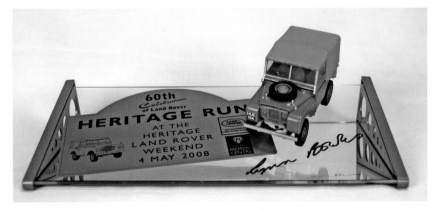

FURTHER READING

Force, Ed. *Corgi Toys.* Schiffer, 2005.

Gardiner, Gordon. *Price Guide to Metal Toys.* Antique Collectors' Club, 1980.

Gardiner, Gordon. *Transport Toys.* Salamander, 1997.

Gardiner, Gordon and Morris, Alistair. *Metal Toys.* Salamander Books, 1984.

Gibson, Cecil. *Commercial Vehicles (Models).* Thomas Nelson, 1970.

Greilsamer, Jacques. *Catalogue of Model Cars of the World.* Edita Lausanne, 1967.

Ramsay, John. *British Diecast Model Toys Catalogue.* Warners Group
Publications plc., 2007.

Tench, Patrick. *Model Cars and Road Vehicles.* Pelham Books, 1983.

Van Cleemput, Marcel R. *The Great Book of Corgi.* New Cavendish Books, 1989.

Williams, Guy. *The World of Model Cars.* André Deutsch, 1976.

PERIODICALS

Collectors' Gazette, Model Collector and *Diecast Collector,* all published monthly,
always feature articles of interest and details of toy fairs and auctions.
Model Buses is published every two months.

PLACES TO VISIT

Intending visitors are advised to check the opening times before travelling
and to find out whether items of particular interest will be on display.

Bressingham Steam Experience, Thetford Road, Bressingham, Diss, Norfolk
IP22 2AB. Telephone: 01379 686900.
Website: www.bressingham.co.uk
Email: info@bressingham.co.uk

Cotswold Motoring Museum and Toy Collection, The Old Mill, Bourton-on-the-
Water, Gloucestershire GL54 2BY.
Telephone: 01451 821255.
Website: www.cotswold-motor-museum.co.uk

Lakeland Motor Museum, Holker Hall and Gardens, Cark-in-Cartmel,
Grange-over-Sands, South Lakeland, Cumbria LA11 7PL.
Telephone: 01539 558509.
Website: www.lakelandmotormuseum.co.uk

Museum of British Road Transport, Hales Street, Coventry CV1 1PN.
Telephone: 024 7623 4270.
Website: www.transport-museum.com

National Motor Museum, John Montagu Building, Beaulieu, Brockenhurst,
Hampshire SO42 7ZN.
Telephone: 01590 612345.
Website: www.beaulieu.co.uk

Romney, Hythe and Dymchurch Toy and Model Museum, New Romney Station, New Romney, Kent TN28 8PL.
Telephone: 01797 362353.
Website: www.rhdr.org.uk
Victoria and Albert Museum of Childhood, Cambridge Heath Road, London E2 9PA.
Telephone: 020 8983 5200.
Website: www.museumofchildhood.org.uk
West Wales Museum of Childhood, Pen-Ffynnon, Llangeler, Carmarthenshire SA44 5EY.
Telephone: 01559 370428.
Website: www.toymuseumwales.co.uk

COLLECTORS' CLUBS AND OTHER ORGANISATIONS
Corgi Collector Club, Meridian East, Meridian Business Park, Leicester LE19 1RL.
Telephone: 0870 607 1204
Email: susie@collectorsclubs.org.uk
Coventry Diecast Model Club (contact: Hugh Evans)
Telephone: 023 7641 9124.
East Anglian Model Car Club, PO Box 60, Norwich NR4 7WB
Email: jnking@ukonline.co.uk
J & J Fairs Ltd (contact: David Webb). Telephone: 01522 698388.
Email: julie.webb2@hotmail.co.uk
Website: j-jwebbtoyfairs.com
Maidenhead Static Model Club (contact: Michael Forbes).
Telephone: 01933 665569.
Vanguards Collector's Club, PO Box 609, Rotherham S60 9AJ
Telephone: 01709 539702.
Wessex Model and Toy Collectors Club (contact: Doug Male)
Telephone: 01225 755043.

INDEX